The Science of Fairy Tales

A Huff-and-Puff Proof House
and the Science of the Three Little Pigs

written by Gloria Koster
illustrated by Daniel Wu

PICTURE WINDOW BOOKS
a capstone imprint

THE SCIENTIFIC METHOD

1. Ask a Question
Ask yourself, "What do I want to learn more about?" or "I wonder what would happen if . . . ?"

2. Form a Hypothesis
Make a prediction or an educated guess about what might happen.

3. Experiment
Test your hypothesis by making a plan and conducting an experiment.

4. Observe and Record
Make careful observations during your experiment and write down what you see.

5. Analyze the Data
Collect and study the results of your data. Was your hypothesis correct?

6. Draw a Conclusion
Make your conclusion and share your results.

Welcome to my home! Don't mind my brother and sister. They live with me. Why do two adults live with their younger brother, you ask? Let me tell you the tale.

Mama kicked us out. It sounds extreme, but it was fair. I'm the baby of the family, and I was 24!

Belle found some straw and built her house in a flash.

Now I can finally relax!

Buster found sticks and threw his house together.

Now I can finally focus on what's important—staying in shape!

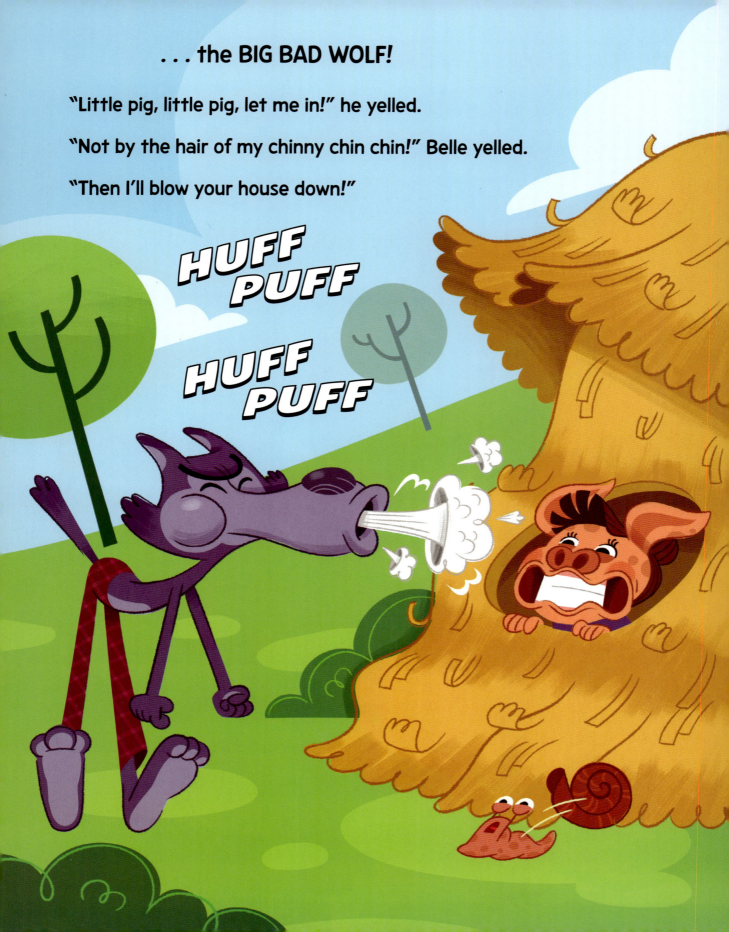

In seconds, the straw house was gone.

Belle ran to Buster's house with the wolf on her tail.

At Buster's house, the same thing happened. Belle and Buster refused to let the wolf inside, but it was no use.

HUFF PUFF HUFF PUFF

In seconds, the stick house was gone.

Belle and Buster raced to my house with the wolf on their tails.

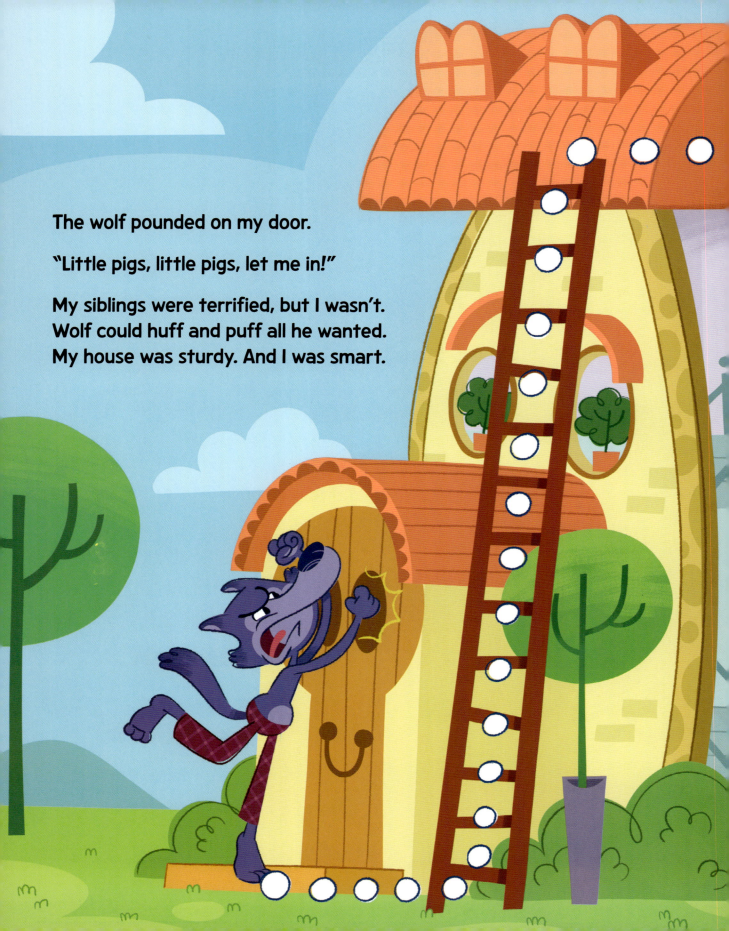

The wolf pounded on my door.

"Little pigs, little pigs, let me in!"

My siblings were terrified, but I wasn't. Wolf could huff and puff all he wanted. My house was sturdy. And I was smart.

I had a pot of stew boiling over the fire. The wolf slid down the chimney—right into the pot.

"Now we guess, or predict, the answer. That's called the **HYPOTHESIS**."

HYPOTHESIS
No. Not all material weighs the same.

EXPERIMENT
Find three different materials.
Use a fan to see if they move.

Belle grabbed a tissue.

Buster grabbed a weight.

I grabbed a plastic cup.

We set everything up next to the fan. I passed out notebooks.

"While we **OBSERVE** the experiment, **RECORD** what you see."

We set the fan to the lowest setting and tested the objects.

Then we set the fan to the highest setting and tested the objects again.

"Now we need to **ANALYZE** the data and draw a **CONCLUSION**," I said.

My siblings studied their notes.

"That tissue flew off the table," Belle said.

"The weight didn't move at all," Buster said.

"And the cup moved a little," I said.

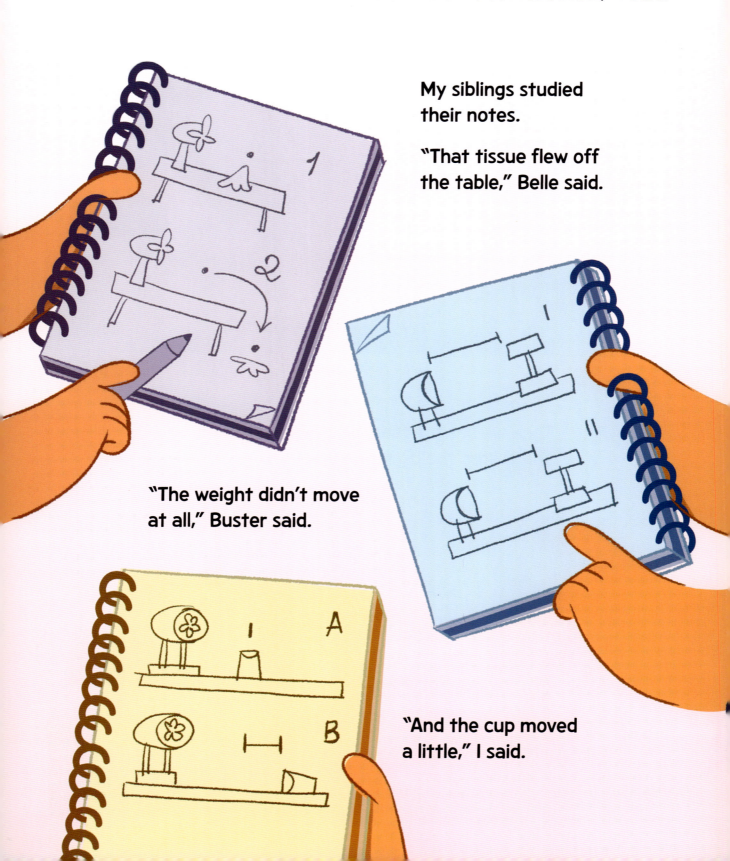

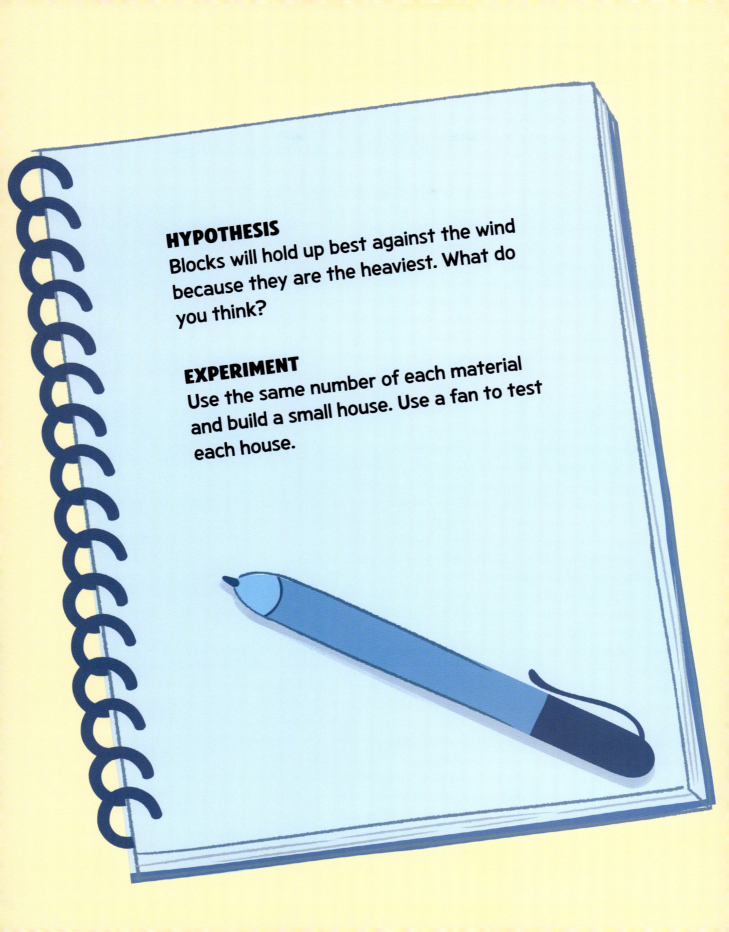

HYPOTHESIS
Blocks will hold up best against the wind because they are the heaviest. What do you think?

EXPERIMENT
Use the same number of each material and build a small house. Use a fan to test each house.

I was so proud of my siblings. They made sure to **OBSERVE** and **RECORD** their data. Then they carefully **ANALYZED** their notes.

"We have our **CONCLUSION!**" Belle announced.

"Our **HYPOTHESIS** was correct," Buster said.

Science proves my house is the safest, which is why my siblings live with me. But I don't mind. It's fun to have science partners.

So what would it take to blow down my house? Could any wolf do it, or is it impossible to blow down a house built of bricks?

You decide!

Do you think the way a house is built affects its strength against wind? Let's use craft sticks and the scientific method to find out.

QUESTION
Can a stick house withstand wind better or worse depending on how it's built?

HYPOTHESIS (Pick one)
No. It will blow down no matter what.
Yes. It can be built to withstand the wind.

EXPERIMENT

Build three different houses using the same materials.

1. Divide 30 craft sticks into three piles of 10.

2. Use tape and creativity to build three different houses.

3. Line up the three houses.

4. Use a fan as your wind source. Start on the low setting.

5. **RECORD** your data. Then repeat on the medium and high settings.

Now **ANALYZE** your data and share your **CONCLUSION**.

What did you discover?

Meet the Author

A public and a school librarian, Gloria Koster belongs to the Children's Book Committee of Bank Street College of Education. She enjoys both city and country life, dividing her time between Manhattan and the small town of Pound Ridge, New York. Gloria has three adult children and a bunch of energetic grandkids.

Photo credit: Domestika

Meet the Illustrator

Daniel Wu is a Brazilian illustrator who loves pizza, chocolate, and making people laugh. He fell in love with children's books as a kid and was amazed by the way they tell stories through pictures. He hasn't stopped drawing since. Daniel creates colorful, expressive characters full of life. His work can be found in games, magazines, and more. He lives in Germany, where he loves exploring Christmas markets.

Published by Picture Window Books, an imprint of Capstone
1710 Roe Crest Drive, North Mankato, Minnesota 56003
capstonepub.com

Copyright © 2026 by Capstone. All rights reserved. No part of this publication may be reproduced in whole or in part, or stored in a retrieval system, or transmitted in any form or by any means, electronic, mechanical, photocopying, recording, or otherwise, without written permission of the publisher.

Library of Congress Cataloging-in-Publication Data is available on the Library of Congress website.

ISBN: 9798875216787 (hardcover)
ISBN: 9798875216732 (paperback)
ISBN: 9798875216749 (ebook PDF)

Summary: The story of the Three Little Pigs is retold by the youngest pig, who uses science to show why his house could withstand the Wolf's huffing and puffing.

Editor: Christianne Jones
Designer: Sarah Bennett
Production Specialist: Katy LaVigne